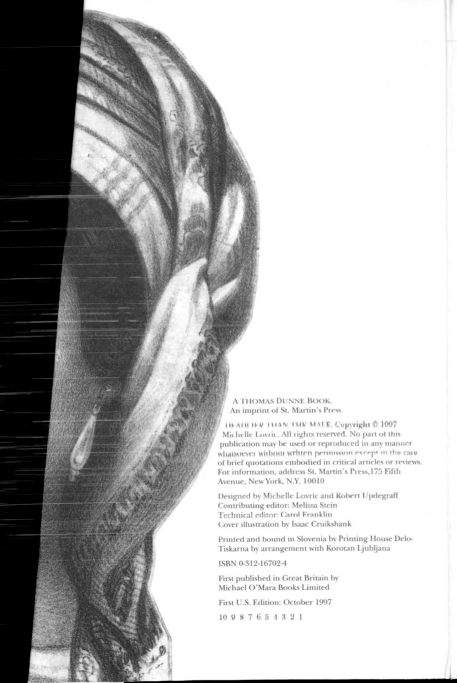

A Thomas Dunne Book.
An imprint of St. Martin's Press.

Designed by Michelle Lovric and Robert Updegraff
Contributing editor: Melissa Stein
Technical editor: Carol Franklin
Cover illustration by Isaac Cruikshank

Printed and bound in Slovenia by Printing House Delo-
Tiskarna by arrangement with Korotan Ljubljana

ISBN 0-312-16702-4

First published in Great Britain by
Michael O'Mara Books Limited

First U.S. Edition: October 1997

10 9 8 7 6 5 4 3 2 1

DEA[
THAN T[

Dangerously W[
by WOMEI

Illustrate[

REGENCY and VICT[

Compiled [
Michelle Lo[

FIGHTING
is essentially
a masculine
idea;
a woman's
weapon
is her
TONGUE.

Hermione Gingold (1897–1987)
English actress

St Martin's Press ☙ New Yo[

CONTENTS

I enjoy vast delight in the folly
of mankind; and, God be
praised, that is an inexhaustible
source of entertainment.

Lady Mary Wortley Montagu (1689–1762)
English woman of letters

Tongue Lashings

I think if women would indulge more freely in vituperation, they would enjoy ten times the health they do. It seems to me they are suffering from repression.

Elizabeth Cady Stanton (1815–1902), American suffragist, abolitionist, historian and writer

OLD MEN, YOUNG MEN, BOYS. PAH! ... THEY FILL ME WITH REPULSION. THERE IS NOTHING IN THE WORLD MORE REPELLENT TO ME, EVEN SMALL BOYS I THINK UNUTTERABLY REPELLENT.

Violet Keppel (1894–1972) English writer

HOW MANY OF YOU EVER STARTED DATING SOMEONE BECAUSE YOU WERE TOO LAZY TO COMMIT SUICIDE?

Judy Tenuta, 20th-century American writer

His mother should have thrown him away and kept the stork.

Mae West (1893–1980), American actress

Jude realized she was feeling awful. She was just back from a week in London at a new biennial Feminist Book Fair... Everywhere you looked, some outraged special-interest group was caucusing. The women of colour were angry at the white women. The working-class women were angry at the middle-class women. The non-English-speaking women were angry at the Anglophones. The lesbians were angry at the heterosexuals. The heterosexuals were angry at the lesbians. And everybody was angry at men.

Lisa Alther (b. 1944), American writer, from Five Minutes in Heaven

"When men speak over-quick and over-fair, what is that but the toadstool that springs from their breath?"

Ouida (Mary Louise de la Ramée) (1839–1908), English novelist, from Folle Farine

Thou ugly filthy camel's face...
Elizabeth, Queen of Bohemia (1596–1662) to James Hay, 1st Earl of Carlisle June 12th, 1630
"His spirit is made of pap, his body of chewed string, and his heart a pumpkin fricasseed in snow."
Quote attributed to Ninon L'Enclos (referring to her lover, the son of Mme de Sévigné) quoted in Madame de Sévigné's letter to her daughter, Mme de Grignan, April 22nd, 1671.

THE WEAKER SEX

The only original thing about some men is original sin.

Helen Rowland (1875–1950)
American journalist

When God created man she was only experimenting.

Graffiti

So, if woman received her crookedness from the rib, and consequently from the Man, how doth man excell in crookedness, who has more of those crooked ribs?

"Ester Sowerman" early 17th-century English writer, from Ester Hath Hang'd Haman, *1619, a reply to* The Arraignment of Lewd, Idle, Forward and Unconstant Woman, *by Joseph Swetnam*

"Well, I've finally figured out that being male is the same thing, more or less, as having a personality disorder."

Carol Shields (b. 1935), American-born Canadian writer from The Republic of Love

Beware of the man who denounces woman writers; his penis is tiny & cannot spell...

Beware of the man who picks your dresses; he wants to wear them.

Erica Jong (b. 1942), American writer

I have had my belly full of great men (forgive the expression). I quite like to read about them in the pages of Plutarch, where they don't outrage my humanity. Let us see them carved in marble or cast in bronze, and hear no more about them. In real life they are nasty creatures, persecutors, temperamental, despotic, bitter and suspicious.

George Sand (Amantine Aurore Dudevant) (1804–76), French writer

A woman is a woman until the day she dies,

Jackie "Moms" Mabley (1894–1975),

But a man's a man only as long as he can.

American singer and comedian

He was not well. Of that fact there could be no doubt. He has been given to hypochondriacal fancies for these last five years, but there was a certain amount of fact underlying these fancies. The effeminately white hand was growing more transparent; the capricious appetite was more difficult to tempt...

Mary Braddon (1837–1915), English novelist, from Asphodel

THE WEAKER SEX

It's not the *men in my life* that counts, it's the *life in my men*.

Mae West (1893–1980), American actress

Since the beginning, the whole feminine world has been in a conspiracy to shield and protect men. Only in fables of chivalry is woman the sheltered sex. Visit any American home and you will find grandmothers, mothers, wives, sisters, aunts, daughters and female servants consecrated to one great purpose – guarding the male members of the family from the vicissitudes of everyday life.

Florence Guy Seabury (1881–1951)
American writer and social commentator

"Men are like snowballs: to begin with, it's a piece of snow, soft and pure and malleable, and easily enough melted; but the snowball soon gets kicked about and mixed up with other snow, and knocked against stones and angles, and hurried, and shoved, and pushed along till, in sheer self-defence, it hardens itself into a solid, impenetrable, immovable block of ice!"

Ouida (Mary Louise de la Ramée) (1839–1908), English novelist
from "Held in Bondage" or Granville de Vigne

If there is anything disagreeable going on, men are sure to get out of it.

Jane Austen (1775–1817), English novelist
from Northanger Abbey

The woman who pins her faith to a man won't find a safety-pin strong enough to stand the strain. *Helen Rowland (1875–1950), American journalist*

For once the girls were speechless. The information they had been given so appalled them
that they wondered how they would ever be
able to bring themselves to marry someone
who owned a thing like a turkey gizzard hidden inside his trousers. And was this really
connected to a John Thomas with a mind of
its own – a feral predatory creature capable of
growing to four times its usual size on sight-
ing a naked woman?

"I will never take my clothes off when I
marry," vowed Theresa fiercely. "Never, *never*."

Sue Reidy, 20th-century New Zealand novelist and designer, from The Visitation

THE WAY MEN LOOK

It is remarkable how little some men can be, how childish, although adorned with hirsute appendages and looking, as far as the outer man goes, intelligent. Yet their talk is all lisped nothings.

from How to Behave, Or, Etiquette of Society, 1879

Naked from the back, Ellen decided, Jack Conroy was more exciting than naked from the front. He was hairy. This man was not born, she thought. He was knitted by his grandmother on a cold day.

Isla Dewar, 20th-century Scottish writer
from Women Talking Dirty

...the yielding Female Lump was with more ease wrought into Perfection, and the curious Line of natural Beauty and Ingenuity; when Man's more rugged knotty Matter could not be carv'd into Excellency without Flaws and Imperfections.

A Preface to the Masculine Sex, by a Young Lady, 1683
from Triumphs of Female Wit in Some Pindaric Odes. Or, the Emulation, together with
an Answer to an Objector against Female Ingenuity, and Capacity of Learning

The man of a family may be, and often is, a very inferior animal to his womankind; made of infinitely poorer, commoner clay; he may be a coarse, surly brute, all body and no soul worth speaking of, or a soul wrapped up and enfolded in swine and turnips, or in gray shirting, or brown sugars, or pill-boxes and blisters.

Rhoda Broughton (1840–1920), English novelist
from Cometh Up As A Flower

When a woman looks at a man in evening dress, she sometimes can't help wondering why he wants to blazon his ancestry to the world by wearing a coat with a long tail to it.

Helen Rowland (1875–1950), American journalist

Although man has learned through evolution to walk in an upright position, his eyes still swing from limb to limb.

Margaret Schooley, 20th-century writer

The Way Men Look

Look at man's uniform drabness, his impersonal envelope! ... The drape of the male is designed to achieve self-forgetfulness.

Carolyn Kizer (b. 1925)
American poet

"I should report him to the advertising standards people for being packaged like a prince and acting like a prat."

Marika Cobbold (b. 1956),
Swedish-English novelist,
from The Purveyor of
Enchantment

A man with a trivial nose should not wear a large moustache. Doing so will increase the insignificance of his insignificant nose ... Sometimes the ends of a man's moustache are visible to persons walking behind him. This imparts to him a belligerent, aggressive air, that makes small children refrain from asking him the time, and saves him from being asked the way by puzzled pedestrians.

Mrs Humphry (?–1925), American writer

His shallowness was as sparkling as the surface of a rivulet.

Mary Braddon (1837–1915)
English novelist,
from Lost for Love

Beware of a mincing step,
whether man or woman.

*Louise Fiske Bryson, 19th-century English writer
from* Every-day Etiquette, 1890

I know there those are who assert, that as the animal powers of the one sex are superior, of course their mental faculties also must be stronger... But if this reasoning is just, man must be content to yield the palm to many of the brute creation, since by not a few of his brethren of the field, he is far surpassed in bodily strength. Moreover, was this argument admitted, it would prove too much, for ocular demonstration evinceth, that there are many robust masculine ladies, and effeminate gentlemen.

Judith Sargent Murray (1751–1820), American feminist writer

[Men who deride women] are commonly either conceited Fops, whose success in their Pretences to the favour of our Sex has been no greater than their Merit, and fallen very far short of their Vanity and Presumption, or a sort of morose, ill-bred, unthinking Fellows, who appear to be Men only by their Habit and Beards, and are scarce distinguishable from Brutes but by their Figure and Risibility.

Judith Drake (fl. 1696), English writer

THE THINGS THEY DON'T UNDERSTAND

> No man can understand why a woman should prefer a good reputation to a good time.
>
> *Helen Rowland (1875–1950)*
> *American journalist*

...for just as women's bodies are softer than men's, so their understanding is sharper.

Christine De Pisan (c.1363–c.1430), French writer

It beats me how Freud could say "What do women want?" as if we must all want the same things.

Katharine Whitehorn (b. 1926), English journalist

He could not believe that she who had loved the dust that his feet had brushed could now regard him as one leprous and accursed. He was slow to understand that his sin had driven him out of her life for evermore.

Ouida (Mary Louise de la Ramée) (1839–1908), English novelist, from Wanda

> I sometimes think that what men really want now is a sexually experienced virgin.
>
> *Anonymous*

When i make love to you
   i try
      with each stroke of my tongue
         to say i love you
         to tease i love you
         to hammer i love you
         to melt i love you

& your sounds drift down
   oh god!
      oh jesus!
   and i think–
here it is, some dude's
getting credit for what
      a woman
      has done,
      again.

Pat Parker (1944–1989), American poet

You can talk to a man about any subject. He won't understand, but you can talk to him. *Anonymous*

When a man can't explain a woman's actions, the first thing he thinks about is the condition of her uterus.

Clare Boothe Luce (1903–87), American diplomat and writer

Even when his heart beat against hers it seemed to him always that there was an invisible wall between himself and her.

Ouida (Mary Louise de la Ramée)
(1839–1908), English novelist
from Wanda

Mr. Gryce's sensations, if less definite, were equally agreeable. He felt his confused titillation with which the lower organisms welcome the gratification of their needs, and all his senses floundered in a vague well-being, through which Miss Bart's personality was dimly but pleasantly perceptible.

Edith Wharton (1862–1937), American writer, from The House of Mirth

Please, God, keep me
from telephoning
him. Please, God.

Dorothy Parker (1893–1967)
American writer

THE PHANTOM MR. RIGHT

There are three kinds of bachelors: the kind that must be driven into matrimony with a whip; the kind that must be coaxed with sugar; and the kind that must be blindfolded and backed into the shafts.

Helen Rowland (1875–1950)
American journalist

With men, Molly was a toad-kisser. She thought any toad could be turned into a prince if only he was kissed enough, by her. I was different. I knew a toad was a toad and would remain so.

Margaret Atwood (b. 1939), Canadian novelist and poet
from Wilderness Tips

No, Mother, I haven't met Mr Right yet ... But I have met Mr Cheap, Mr Rude, and Mr Married.
T-shirt

I have been this ten days in debate whether I should hang or marry, in which time I have cried some two hours every day and knocked my head against the wall some fifteen times.

Lady Mary Wortley Montagu (1689–1762), English woman of letters, in a letter to her friend, Miss Philippa Mundy, November 2nd, 1711.

THE PHANTOM MR RIGHT

At a successful dance there must be at least three men to every girl. The result is that almost any trousered thing is called in to make up the stag line.

Alice-Leone Moats (1908–89), American journalist and writer

Miss Penruth was now nine-and-thirty years of age. She had dismissed the last of her lovers with a fretful sense of disappointment, but with no real grief; and she had made up her mind to die unmated. She had essayed various specimens of humanity, and found them all wanting. She had tried the gold, the silver, and the leaden casket, and had discovered emptiness in all.

Mary Braddon (1837–1915), English novelist from
The Story of Barbara, Her Splendid Misery, and her Gilded Cage

But how tired Effie was of balls! She had been to so many in her life, had danced so unceasingly in pursuit of an ever-vanishing husband. She had been trying to look arch, and pretty, and lively, for exactly twelve years... It was the old, old tragi-comedy; the degrading, unceasing pursuit of the possible husband.

Ella Hepworth Dixon (1857–1932), English writer
from One Doubtful Hour, and Other Side-Lights on the Feminine Temperament

It is sad but true that the more amusing the young man, the less apt he is to telephone a girl after their first meeting.

Alice-Leone Moats (1908–89)
American journalist and writer

"The point is" – she shook her head – "I couldn't possibly marry a man I laughed at. Surely you see that. The man I marry –" breathed Anne softly. She broke off. She drew her hand away, and ... she smiled strangely, dreamily. "The man I marry –"

And it seemed to Reggie that a tall, handsome, brilliant stranger stepped in front of him and took his place – the kind of man that Anne and he had seen often at the theatre, walking on to the stage from nowhere, without a word catching the heroine in his arms, and after one long, tremendous look, carrying her off to anywhere...

Katherine Mansfield (1888–1923), New Zealand-born British writer, from The Garden Party

THE PHANTOM

She had been bored all the afternoon by Percy Gryce – the mere thought seemed to waken an echo of his droning voice – but she could not ignore him on the morrow, she must follow up her success, must submit to more boredom, must be ready with fresh compliances and adaptabilities, and all on the bare chance that he might ultimately decide to do her the honour of boring her for life.

Edith Wharton (1862–1937), American writer
from The House of Mirth

She had no idea that the hopeless gaze of those mild blue eyes meant idolatry; she ascribed their pensively imploring expression to constitutional weakness.

Mary Braddon (1837–1915), English novelist
from Sir Jasper's Tenant

I am tired
of being a
free
finishing school
for *men*.

Suzanne Wolstenholme (1946–95), English designer

She felt her heart go liquid, but she did her best to be harder won.

Dorothy Parker (1893–1967), American writer
from Dusk Before Fireworks

MR RIGHT

Indeed he has all the qualities that would make a husband tolerable – battlement, veranda, stable, etc., no grins and no glass in his eye.

George Eliot (Mary Ann Evans) (1819–80), English novelist, from Daniel Deronda

Many are saved from sin by being so inept at it.

Mignon McLaughlin, 20th-century American writer

Eleanor's three offers were so absurdly free from preliminary love-making, that she must be excused for not having foreseen and prevented them.

Annie Victoria Dutton, 19th-century English writer from Wisdom's Folly. A Study in Feminine Development

Hugh never thought it necessary to lower his voice when he said anything tender. The expression "love whisper" never could be applied to his amatory commonplaces; love-shout or love-bellow would be more applicable.

Rhoda Broughton (1840–1920), English novelist, from Cometh Up as A Flower

Whether it was all love and no champagne, or all champagne and no love, or half love and half champagne, or three quarters love and a quarter champagne, or one quarter love and three quarters champagne, I cannot say; but certain it is that Hugh be inconveniently tender.

Rhoda Broughton (1840 1920), English novelist, from Cometh Up as A Flower

Only once did he inspire a momentary interest and excitement in Eleanor, and that was an unlucky moment for him.

Annie Victoria Dutton, 19th-century English writer, from Wisdom's Folly. A Study in Feminine Development

Men are creatures with two legs and eight hands.

Jayne Mansfield (1932–67), American actress

Utterly innocent in her utter ignorance of evil, she saw no snare in such simple joys, she had no premonition of danger. Her worst suspicion of the stranger was that he might be poor.

Mary Braddon (1837–1915), English novelist, from Asphodel

THE VILE SEDUCER

American men look at women when [they think] the women are not aware of it; Englishmen do not look at them at all; but Frenchmen look at them with such thoroughness and intensity that you half expect them to approach and ask dubiously, "Is it washable?"

Margaret Halsey (b. 1910), American novelist, critic and humourist
from With Malice Toward Some

It appears difficult for masculine mentality to grasp the difference between living alone and living loosely.

Alice-Leone Moats (1908–89)
American journalist and writer

It occurs to her that men do not look at a woman with women's eyes. Men, being three parts animal themselves, condone any offence in a woman the animal part of whom is perfect and beautiful.

Rhoda Broughton (1840–1920), English novelist
from As Red as a Rose is She

The one thing about love-making that the modern man simply can't understand is that, in order to make it thrilling and interesting, he must really put a little *love* in it.

Helen Rowland (1875–1950), American journalist

And in these eyes the love-light lies

Anita Owen (fl. 1890s)

A woman must keep her conscience, her complexion and her reputation snow-white. But a man is satisfied if he can just manage to keep his so that they comply with the pure food laws.

Helen Rowland (1875–1950), American journalist

The perception that poor Rex wanted to be tender made her curl up and harden like a sea-anemone at the touch of a finger.

George Eliot (Mary Ann Evans) (1819–80), English novelist from Daniel Deronda

"Men are ugly. They are dirty. They say, 'Come here, my little girl, and I will give you something' – then when I go to them they will try and kiss me. And I will not kiss them, because their mouths smell bad. They stroke my hair and pull it all the wrong way; and it hurts. And when I don't like my hair pulled the wrong way, they tell me I will be a great coquette."

Marie Corelli (Mary Mackay) (1855–1924), English popular romantic novelist

The only way to avoid being picked up is to develop the psychology of the averted eye.

Alice-Leone Moats (1908–89) American journalist and writer

And lies — and lies and lies!

American poet

Give a man a free hand
and he'll run it all over you.

Mae West (1893–1980), American actress

THE VILE SEDUCER

Though woman needs the protection of one man against his whole sex, in pioneer life, in threading her way through a lonely forest, on the highway, or in the streets of the metropolis on a dark night, she sometimes needs, too, the protection of all men against this one.

Elizabeth Cady Stanton (1815–1902)
American suffragist, abolitionist, historian and writer

"He would not touch Amaryllis with a pair of tongs," cry I.

Rhoda Broughton (1840–1920)
English novelist
from Cometh Up as A Flower

What, love a rake, a man of professed gallantry? impossible. – To me, a common rake is as odious, as a common prostitute is to a man of the nicest feelings. – Where can be the pride of inspiring a passion, fifty others can equally inspire? or the transport of bestowing favours, where the appetite is already cloyed by fruition of the self-same enjoyments?

Elizabeth Inchbald (1753–1821), English writer and actress, from A Simple Story

Vane Castleton had gone mad about Alma. I do not mean that he loved her ... but he was wild about her, as very heartless men, *chères demoiselles,* can be wild about a woman who has bewitched them ... if he had been in the East he would have sent his slaves, had her blindfolded, and kept her in his seraglio, without regard as to whether tears or smiles were the consequences.

Ouida (Mary Louise de la Ramée) (1839–1908), English novelist
from "Held in Bondage" *or* Granville de Vigne

"Off! do not touch me!" cried Alma, fiercely, as his hand wandered towards the delicate form that he could crush in his grasp as a tiger's fangs a young gazelle. "Your words are shame, your love pollution, your presence hateful! Insult me no more ... I shall never be yours – dastard! – coward!' gasped she ... as she struggled in the iron grasp of his embrace, maddened by the loathsome kisses he banded on her lips – abhorred caresses that seemed to pollute her with infamy and shame.

Ouida (Mary Louise de la Ramée) (1839–1908), English novelist from "Held in Bondage" or Granville de Vigne

The flood was rising up in him – higher, higher – taking giant steps fiercer than ever it surged and boiled; he *could* not stand it any longer. It was stronger than he. Devils are mightier than men. What good wasting one's strength wrestling with them? He gave in.

Rhoda Broughton (1840–1920), English novelist from Not Wisely But Too Well

The offer of a man's heart and hand is the greatest compliment he can pay you, and, however undesirable to you those gifts may be, they should be courte-ously and kindly declined... Men have various ways of cherish-ing and declaring their attach-ment; those who indicate the bias of their feel-ings in many intelligible ways can generally be spared the pain of a refusal.

Flora Klickmann (1867–1958), English journalist and writer from How to Behave, A Handbook of Etiquette for All

There are two kinds of passes: the verbal and the physical. The first can be easily overlooked, as it need never be understood; but the second, alas, is always too clear to admit of any misunderstanding. Direct measures are required, and it is not always easy to escape a gentle-man's too pressing attentions with tact as well as firmness. Evasiveness and flippancy are the best weapons – if they work. Of course, if you never wish to see the man again, you can use the direct rebuff, or the kicking and screaming method. But even that fails if you happen to draw a rough-and-tumble type. If you can get away with the "Sir, you've insulted me" attitude, by all means adopt it. We never could.

Alice-Leone Moats (1908–89), American journalist and writer

To bringe a woman to offend in one sinne, how many damnable sinnes doe they commit?

"Ester Sowerman" early 17th-century English writer from Ester Hath Hang'd Haman, *1619, a reply to* The Arraignment of Lewd, Idle, Forward and unconstatnt Woman, *by Joseph Swetnam*

No darling – it only leads to housework.
Graffiti

She took good care never to be alone with him, even for a few minutes, lest he should break out again.

Mary Braddon (1837–1915) English novelist from Lost for Love

THE MARITAL VOYAGE

OLINDA ... this marrying I do not like: 'tis like going on a long voyage to sea, where after a while even the calms are distasteful, and the storms dangerous: one seldom sees a new object, 'tis still a deal of sea, sea, husband, husband, every day, – till one's quite cloyed with it.

Aphra Behn (1640–89), English novelist, dramatist and poet, from The Dutch Lover

Having once embarked on your marital voyage, it is impossible not to be aware that you make no way and that the sea is not within sight – that, in fact, you are exploring an enclosed basin.

George Eliot (Mary Ann Evans) (1819–80), English novelist, from Middlemarch

Women who have fostered a romantic unnatural delicacy of feeling, waste their lives in *imagining* how happy they should have been with a husband who could love them with a fervid increasing affection every day, and all day. But they might as well pine married as single.

Mary Wollstonecraft (1759–97), English writer

The state of matrimony is a dangerous disease: far better to take drink in my opinion.

Madame de Sévigné (1626–96), French salonist and letter writer

"I'd rather be flayed alive! Ugh! married to Hugh! I should be dead of disgust in a week! Faugh!"

Rhoda Broughton (1840–1920), English novelist from, Cometh Up as A Flower

When you see what some girls marry, you realize how they must hate to work for a living.

Helen Rowland (1875–1950), American journalist

I married beneath me, all women do.

Nancy Astor (1879–1964), English politician

Alas! In choosing a husband, it seems that you've always got to decide between something tame and uninteresting, like a goldfish, and something wild and fascinating, like a mountain goat.

Helen Rowland (1875–1950), American journalist

Some women govern their husbands without degrading themselves, because intellect will always govern.

Mary Wollstonecraft (1759–97), English writer

"Mr Vanderdecken?" said Lady Dolly, waking to fact. "Oh, he is on the sea going somewhere. He is always going somewhere; it is Java or Japan, or Jupiter; something with a J. He makes money in that sort of way, you know. I never understand it myself. Whenever people want money he goes, and he makes it because the people he goes to haven't got any; isn't it queer?"

Ouida (Mary Louise de la Ramée) (1839–1908), English novelist, from Moths

The only danger is that the Wife be more knowing than the Husband; but if she be, 'tis his own fault, since he wants no opportunities for improvement; unless he be a natural Blockhead, and then such an one will need a wise Woman to govern him, whose prudence will conceal it from publick Observation, and at once both cover and supply his defects.

Mary Astell (1666–1731), English writer

Alas! for all the pretty women who marry dull men,
Go into the suburbs and never come out again...

Anna Wickham (1884–1947), English poet

* 33 *

DOMESTIC VICISSITUDES

My heart almost broke with the cruel thought that our marriage is based upon the cold, stern word duty.

Lucretia Rudolph Garfield (1832–1918)
American first lady

"Is *this* the man whose *mind* I have married? Is this the man who is to teach me to live by the intellect? Is this the scholar and the sage, whose teaching was to lift me out of the circle of my narrow interests into the sphere of the Universal?" she asks with contemptuous misgivings; *"this*, whose whole soul is occupied by mean parsimonies, and economies of cheese-rinds and candle-ends?"

Rhoda Broughton (1840–1920), English novelist
from Belinda

Was it her fault that she had believed in him – had believed in his worthiness? – And what, exactly, was he? – She was able enough to estimate him – she who waited on his glances with trembling, and shut her best soul in prison, paying it only hidden visits, that she might be petty enough to please him. In such a crisis as this, some women begin to hate.

George Eliot (Mary Ann Evans), (1819–80) English novelist, from Middlemarch

Roland has the inner life of a tree, or possibly of a stump.

Margaret Atwood (b. 1939), Canadian novelist and poet, from Wilderness Tips

For a pair of first-class blue eyes warranted a fast colour, for ditto superfine red lips, for so many pounds of prime white flesh, he has paid down a handsome price on the nail, without any haggling, and now if he may not test the worth of his purchases, poor man, he *is* hardly used! As for me, I sit tolerable still, and am not yet actually sick.

Rhoda Broughton (1840–1920), English novelist, from Cometh Up As A Flower

Though I know he loves me,

Tonight my heart is sad;

His kiss was not so wonderful

As all the dreams I had.

Sara Teasdale (1884–1933), American poet from The Kiss

DOMESTIC VICISSITUDES

> I am happy now that Charles calls on my bedchamber less frequently ... when I hear his steps outside my door I lie down on my bed, close my eyes, open my legs and think of England.
>
> *Lady Hillingdon (1857–1940), English aristocrat and writer*

And when her biographer says of an Italian woman poet, "during some years her Muse was intermitted," we do not wonder at the fact when he casually mentions her ten children.

Anna Garlin Spencer (1851–1931), American minister, social reformer, educator and feminist

Estimated from a wife's experience, the average man spends fully one-quarter of his life in looking for his shoes.

Helen Rowland (1875–1950) American journalist

Love is a farce; matrimony is a humbug; husbands are domestic Napoleons, Neroes, Alexanders, – sighing for other hearts to conquer, after they are sure of yours. The honeymoon is as short-lived as a lucifer-match; after that you may wear your wedding-dress at the wash tub, and your night-cap to meeting, and your husband wouldn't know it. You may pick up your own pocket-handkerchief, help yourself to a chair, and split your gown across the back reaching over the table to get a piece of butter, while he is laying into his breakfast as if it was the last meal he should eat this side of Jordan... Then he gets up from the table, lights his cigar with the last evening's paper, that you have not had a chance to read; gives two or three whiffs of smoke, – which are sure to give you a headache for the forenoon, – and, just as his coat-tail is vanishing through the door, apologizes for not doing "that errand" for you yesterday, – thinks it doubtful if he can to-day, – "so *pressed with business.*" Hear of him at eleven o'clock, taking an ice-cream with some ladies at a confectioner's, while you are new-lining his old coat-sleeves. Children by the ears all day, can't get out to take the air, feel as crazy as a fly in a drum; husband comes home at night, nods a "How d'ye do, Fan," boxes Charley's ears, stands little Fanny in the corner, sits down in the easiest chair in the warmest corner, puts his feet up over the grate, shutting out all the fire, while the baby's little pug nose grows blue with the cold; reads the newspaper all to himself, solaces his inner man with a hot cup of tea, and, just as you are labouring under the hallucination that he will ask you to take a mouthful of fresh air with him, he puts on his dressing-gown and slippers, and begins to reckon up the family expenses! after which he lies down on the sofa, and you keep time with your needle, while he sleeps till nine o'clock.

Fanny Fern (Sara Payson Willis Parton) (1811–72), American writer

When he is late for dinner and I know he must be either having an affair or lying dead on the street, I always hope he's dead.

Judith Viorst (b. 1931), American writer, poet and journalist

Why should marriage bring only tears?
All I wanted was a man
With a single heart,
And we would stay together
As our hair turned white,
Not somebody always after wriggling fish
With his big bamboo rod.

Chuo Wên-chün (179–117 BC), Chinese poet and legendary lover

SEXUAL MISDEMEANOURS

A
WOMAN'S
HEART
ALWAYS
HAS
A
BURNED
MARK.

*Louise Labé
(1524/5–66), French
poet, linguist, feminist
and soldier*

IN LOVE,

AS

IN PAIN,

IN SHOCK,

IN TROUBLE.

*Germaine Greer (b. 1939)
Australian-born feminist,
critic and journalist*

The tragedy of Lady Llanbister's girlhood was but the common story of a woman's confiding love and a man's treason. It was only the seducer's rank and the victim's noble character which distinguished the history of this case,,, Viola Redgrave passed from the monotony of a joyless girlhood to the tempest and passion of a fatal love.

*Mary Braddon (1837–1915), English novelist
from* In High Places

To adulterous lust the most sacred duties are sacrificed, because before marriage, men, by a promiscuous intimacy with women, learned to consider love as a selfish gratification – learned to separate it not only from esteem, but from the affection merely built on habit, which mixes a little humanity with it.

Mary Wollstonecraft (1759–97), English writer

Beware of loving a man. Today he says, "I love you, I need you! I shall go to the devil without you!" Tomorrow he turns to his affairs. In six months he says, "I was a fool!" Next year he says, "Who was it that drove me wild for a time last year? What was her name?"

Mary Hartwell Catherwood (1847–1901), American writer

Does a ring and a ceremony instantly convert a man, who is that most selfish and obdurate of all sinners – a libertine? Ill betide the woman who pins her happiness on such a creed... You believe, perhaps, in the converting power of your own charms! why, if you were (blended in one charming tout le ensemblé,) Cleopatra, Ninon, Mary Stuart, in beauty and fascination, how could you hope to chain men, the very essence of whom is variety?

Augusta Johnstone, 19th-century English writer

WICKED BRUTES

Father's temper got up despert quick, and when it was up he was a ravening lion.

Mary Webb (1881–1927), English writer, from Precious Bane

Ah, when one thinks what a miserable creature man is! Every other animal can, at his will, wear on his face the expression he pleases. He is not obligated to smile if he has a mind to weep. When he does not wish to see his fellows he does not see them. While man is the slave of everything and everybody!

Marie Konstantinovna Bashkirtseff (1860–84), Russian artist and diarist

I DON'T KNOW HOW MEN ARE DIFFERENT FROM HOGS ... THEY CHASE AFTER THE SAME THINGS: FOOD, DRINK, WOMEN.

Emilia Pardo Bazán (1852–1921), Spanish novelist, educator, stateswoman and feminist

What littleness of mind! what an unfeeling and despicable meanness must lurk in the breasts of those, who can, with impunity, insult over distress! Into what fits of desperation have numbers of helpless females fallen through these contemptible insults and reviling, and even neglects! for, it is in those dark moments of distress, when the senses are all alive to the fine feelings of nature, that every nerve is relaxed and ready to receive the fatal dart.

Mary Anne Radcliffe (1764–1823), English writer

MEN ARE BEASTS, AND EVEN BEASTS DON'T BEHAVE AS THEY DO.

Brigitte Bardot (b. 1934) French actress

....Masculine tenderness is said to respond to tears. I do not find it so. Rather, I should say that a man's devotion fades under salt water, like a bathing-suit in the very element for which it is supposed to be adapted.

Mary Adams, 19th-century American writer

MEN AND DOGS:

It is well to love even a dog when you have the opportunity, for fear you should find nothing else worth loving.

Louise Honorine de Choiseul (1734–1801)
French letter writer

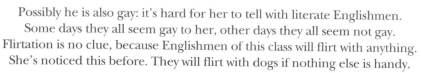

Let us love dogs; let us love only dogs! Men and cats are unworthy creatures...

Marie Konstantinovna Bashkirtseff (1860–84), Russian artist and diarist

Possibly he is also gay: it's hard for her to tell with literate Englishmen. Some days they all seem gay to her, other days they all seem not gay. Flirtation is no clue, because Englishmen of this class will flirt with anything. She's noticed this before. They will flirt with dogs if nothing else is handy.

Margaret Atwood (b. 1939), Canadian novelist and poet, from Wilderness Tips

Oh girls! set your affections on cats, poodles, parrots or lap dogs; but let matrimony alone. It's the hardest way on earth of getting a living.

Fanny Fern (Sara Payson Willis Parton) (1811–72), American writer

UNFAIR COMPARISONS

The more I see of men,
the more I like dogs.

*Germaine de Staël (1766–1817) French
woman of letters*

OLD WRECKS

It was with real sorrow that he saw the beautiful young head leaning so near the high, narrow forehead, prematurely bald and deeply lined – the fresh and pure cheek of girlhood almost touching the cheek of wasted manhood, with its livid, bloodless hue and sunken outline. "Women are like barnacles," he said; "they are always ready to fasten upon a wreck."

Mary Braddon (1837–1915), English novelist from One Life, One Love

An old man can't do nothing for me · except bring me a message from a young man ·

Jackie "Moms" Mabley (1894–1975) American singer and comedian

"For a man of my age, Venus, the implacable goddess, transforms herself into a nursing sister, and Cupid changes his venomous arrows into the spoon that stirs an invalid's messes of beef-tea and barley-water. A man of my age is not entirely a useless twaddler, for upon him lovely woman can practise and bring to perfection the arts by which she may hereafter subjugate her youthful adorers. It is only at my time of life, when love would be an imbecility and marriage an act of dotage, that a man can derive unalloyed enjoyment from feminine society."

Mary Braddon (1837–1915), English novelist, from Sir Jasper's Tenant

The old squire is a superb wreck. Spiteful Time is fond of removing the landmarks that youth sets upon our faces; is fond of changing great, clear, almond eyes into little damp jellies – sweet, moist purse-mouths into dry bags of wrinkles...

Rhoda Broughton (1840–1920), English novelist, from As Red as a Rose is She

MEN ARE ... SELFISH

The lust of dominion was probably the first effect of the fall; and as there was no other intelligent being over whom to exercise it, woman was the first victim of this unhallowed passion... All history attests that man has subjected woman to his will, used her as a means to promote his selfish gratification, to minister to his sensual pleasures, to be instrumental in promoting his comfort; but never has he desired to elevate her to that rank she was created to fill. He has done all he could to debase and enslave her mind; and now he looks triumphantly on the ruin he has wrought, and says, the being he has thus deeply injured is his inferior.

Sarah Moore Grimké (1792–1873), American reformer, from Letters on the Equality of the Sexes

"Before he was married" his handkerchiefs were always laid in a pile in the northeast corner of his drawer, duly perfumed, and with the exquisite word *"Augustus"* embroidered in the corner. – And *now!* "Before he was married" he was always consulted about the number of plums in his pudding. – And *now!* "Before he was married" he was never bothered to wait upon a woman of an evening unless he chose. – And *now!* "Before he was married" he had his breakfast any time between seven in the morning and three in the afternoon. – And *now!*

And so the poor weary woman hears the changes rung upon the newly-discovered virtues and perfections of his family, till she heartily wishes he had never left them. It never once occurs meanwhile to the domestic Nero to look at the *other* side of the question. How should it? when all his life at home was one ovation to his vanity and selfishness.

Fanny Fern (Sara Payson Willis Parton) (1811–72), American writer

...all the lovers I have had have invariably begun by talking of my interests, and telling me that they loved my life, my welfare, and my honour, and the upshot of it all has no less invariably been their own inter-est, their own pleasure, and their own vanity.

Marguerite of Navarre (1492–1549)
French poet, author, religious
reformer and Queen

Rejoice, and men will seek you;
  Grieve, and they turn and go.
They want full measure
  of all your pleasure.

Ella Wheeler Wilcox (1850–1919)
American journalist and poet

"I wandered lonely as a ...
They're in the top drawer, William,
Under your socks –
I wandered lonely as a –
No not that drawer, the top one.
I wandered by myself –
Well wear the ones you can find,
No, don't get overwrought my dear,
I'm coming.

"I was out one day wandering
Lonely as a cloud when
Softboiled egg, yes my dear,
As usual, three minutes –
As a cloud when all of a sudden –
Look, I said I'll cook it,
Just hold on will you –
All right, I'm coming.

"One day I was out for a walk
When I saw this flock –
It can't be too hard, it had three minutes.
Well put some butter in it.
– This host of golden daffodils
As I was out for a stroll one –

"Oh you fancy a stroll, do you.
Yes, all right William. I'm coming.
It's on the peg. Under your hat.
I'll bring my pad, shall I, in case
You want to jot something down?"

Lynn Peters (b. 1953), English journalist, poet

I am more and more convinced
that man is a dangerous creature
and that power, whether vested in
many or a few, is ever grasping, and
like the grave, cries "Give, Give!"

Abigail Adams (1744–1818), American first lady and feminist

The hen knows when it is daybreak but allows the

A bachelor never quite gets over the idea that he is

Helen Rowland (1875–1950)
American journalist

The intelligent man who is proud of his intelligence is
like thc condemned man who is proud of his large cell.

Simone Weil (1909–43), French philosopher, mystic and writer

MEN ARE

rooster to make the announcement

a thing of beauty and a boy forever.

Ashanti Proverb

"As to his ever falling in love," thought the young lady sometimes, "the idea is too preposterous. If all the divinities upon earth were ranged before him, waiting for his sultanship to throw the handkerchief, he would only lift his eyebrows to the middle of his forehead and left them to scramble for it."

Mary Braddon (1837–1915)
English novelist
from Lady Audley's Secret

She had rightly guessed that Mr. Gryce's egoism was a thirsty soil, requiring constant nurture from without.

Edith Wharton (1862–1937), American writer, from The House of Mirth

... VAIN

MEN ARE ...
POWER-CRAZED

Poor Mary Ann! She gave the guy an inch and now he thinks he's a ruler.

Mae West (1893–1980), American actress

I am unable to learn from sacred writ when woman was deprived by God of her equality with man...

Sarah Moore Grimké (1792–1873) American reformer

If all men are born free, how is it that all women are born slaves?

Mary Astell (1666–1731) English writer

"If a woman had split the atom and unleashed that power she would have taken it to other women. To Helena Rubenstein or Coco Chanel and told them to see what they could do in the way of producing the ultimate moisturiser."

Isla Dewar, 20th-century Scottish writer, from Women Talking Dirty

Ye simple men! so tenacious of your prerogative, insinuate yourselves gently into our affections and understandings, respect in us the majesty of rationality, upon which ye so fully value yourselves, and ye will have no cause to complain that like wayward children, spoilt by equally misjudged caresses and correction, we in fact tyrannise over you by our caprices, while you are deluded with mock ensigns of power.

Mary Hays (1760–1843), English feminist and radical

Eric is sitting at the kitchen table having his morning rage.

Margaret Atwood (b. 1939), Canadian novelist and poet, from Wilderness Tips

Belinda has not yet got into the habit of being married. There still seems to her something improbable – nay monstrous – in the fact of herself sitting opposite to Professor Forth at breakfast in their Folkestone lodgings, pouring weak tea for him out of a Britannia metal teapot, and sedulously recollecting how many lumps of sugar he likes, as she has already discovered that he has an objection to repeating the information. Nor is it less monstrous to be warming his overcoat, and cutting his newspapers, and ordering his dinners with that nice attention to digestibility and economy which she finds to be expected of her. They have been enormously long, these three days.

Rhoda Broughton (1840–1920), English novelist, from Belinda

MEN ARE ... PATRONIZING

Elizabeth would be the easiest woman in the world to manage. How is it that in her ten years of womanhood no man has been found to undertake the lovely facile task? He himself knows perfectly the treatment that would befit her; the hinted wishes – her tact is too fine and her spirit too meek to need anything so coarse as commands – the infinitesimal rebukes and the unlimited – oh! limitless – caresses...

Rhoda Broughton (1840–1920), English novelist, from Alas!

Of anything that could be called mind in a woman Tony had a dislike which was akin to absolute fear...

Mary Braddon (1837–1915), English novelist from Under Love's Rule

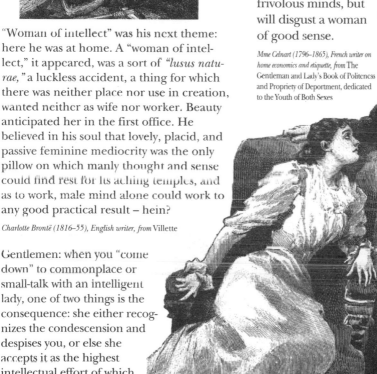

A learned woman is thought to be a comet, that bodes mischief when she appears.

Bathsua Makin (1612–74), English scholar and writer

It is bad *ton* to overwhelm with insipid flattery, all women that we meet, without distinction of age, rank or merit. It may indeed please some of light and frivolous minds, but will disgust a woman of good sense.

Mme Celnart (1796–1865), French writer on home economics and etiquette, from The Gentleman and Lady's Book of Politeness and Propriety of Deportment, dedicated to the Youth of Both Sexes

"Woman of intellect" was his next theme: here he was at home. A "woman of intellect," it appeared, was a sort of *"lusus naturae,"* a luckless accident, a thing for which there was neither place nor use in creation, wanted neither as wife nor worker. Beauty anticipated her in the first office. He believed in his soul that lovely, placid, and passive feminine mediocrity was the only pillow on which manly thought and sense could find rest for its aching temples, and as to work, male mind alone could work to any good practical result – hein?

Charlotte Brontë (1816–55), English writer, from Villette

Gentlemen: when you "come down" to commonplace or small-talk with an intelligent lady, one of two things is the consequence: she either recognizes the condescension and despises you, or else she accepts it as the highest intellectual effort of which you are capable, and rates you accordingly.

Mrs E. B. Duffey, 19th-century American writer, from The Ladies' and Gentlemen's Etiquette, 1877

So It's War

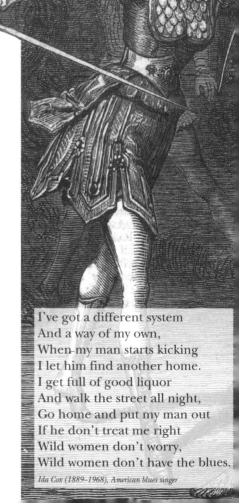

We will meet upon even ground, the despot man; we will rush with alacrity to the combat, and, crowned by success, we shall then answer the exalted expectations which are formed. Though sensibility, soft compassion, and gentle commiseration are inmates in the female bosom, yet against every deep-laid art, altogether fearless of the event, we will set them in array; for assuredly the wreath of victory will encircle the spotless brow.

Judith Sargent Murray (1751–1820), American feminist writer

THE VOTE, I THOUGHT, MEANS NOTHING TO WOMEN. WE SHOULD BE ARMED.

Edna O'Brien (b. 1932), Irish writer

I am calling upon my sex to sacrifice what has been, what is still dear to their hearts, the adulation, the flattery, the attentions of trifling men. I am asking them to repel these insidious enemies whenever they approach them.

Sarah Moore Grimké (1792–1873), American reformer

Husband and wife gazed steadily at each other without a word. No word was needed, for in that look there passed, like a sword-thrust, the vision of an eternal rancour.

Ella Hepworth Dixon (1857–1932) English writer
from "The World's Slow Stain", – One Doubtful Hour, and Other Side-Lights on the Feminine Temperament

I've got a different system
And a way of my own,
When my man starts kicking
I let him find another home.
I get full of good liquor
And walk the street all night,
Go home and put my man out
If he don't treat me right
Wild women don't worry,
Wild women don't have the blues.

Ida Cox (1889–1968), American blues singer

Prince Zouroff had a horror of unmarried women.

Ouida (Mary Louise de la Ramée) (1839–1908) English novelist, from Moths

He couldn't see a belt without hitting below it.

Margot Asquith (1865–1945), English writer

Study the weak part of the character of your enemy – your husband I mean: if he be a man of high spirit, jealous of command, and impatient of control; one who decides for himself, and is little troubled with the insanity of minding what the world says of him, you must proceed with extreme circumspection; you must not dare to provoke the combined forces of the enemy to a regular engagement, but harrass him with perpetual petty skirmishes, in these, though you gain little at a time, you will gradually weary the patience, and break the spirit of your opponent.

Maria Edgeworth (1767–1849), Irish novelist and essayist

This man here will dismiss it as spite or aggravation or at least as mere obstinacy when a women disagrees with his opinion, no matter how discreet she tries to be, either because he does not believe that women can disturb his precious mind by any means other than spite and obstinacy or because he feels deep inside his heart that he is poorly prepared for the battle and needs to start a silly quarrel about nothing in order to get out of it.

Marie de Gournay (1565–1645), French writer

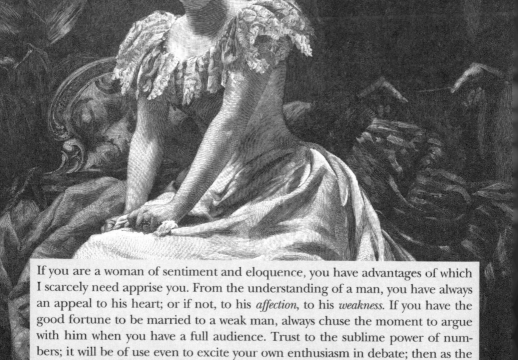

Bob is not of a suspicious nature, but he can add two and two together. He has been doing that little dreary sum all the last ten days, till his head aches.

Rhoda Broughton (1840–1920), English novelist
from As Red as a Rose is She

If you are a woman of sentiment and eloquence, you have advantages of which I scarcely need apprise you. From the understanding of a man, you have always an appeal to his heart; or if not, to his *affection*, to his *weakness*. If you have the good fortune to be married to a weak man, always chuse the moment to argue with him when you have a full audience. Trust to the sublime power of numbers; it will be of use even to excite your own enthusiasm in debate; then as the scene advances, talk of his cruelty, and your sensibility, and sink with "becoming woe," into the pathos of *injured innocence*.

Maria Edgeworth (1767–1849), Irish novelist and essayist

IT'S WAR

A new searching light had fallen on her husband's character, and she could not judge him leniently.

George Eliot (Mary Ann Evans) (1819–80), English novelist, from Middlemarch

When she settled down for a life-time's quarrelling at him, it was for the same reason syrup sours — the heat had just been put to her too long.

Marjorie Kinnan Rawlings (1896–1953), American writer, from When the Whippoorwill

"I was his chattel as much as his pet lean-headed mare... Sometimes I will confess to you that I wished he would transfer his amities to some other person, even if it were the cook... All Sir Hugh's other servants, if they disliked their situations, or got tired of them, might give warning and leave; but I, however wearied I might be of mine, could never give warning, could never leave. I was a fixture for life. So I said to myself sometimes, and ground my teeth, and snarled like a caged tiger."

*Rhoda Broughton (1840–1920)
English novelist
from* Cometh Up as A Flower

I like your Plan immensely of Extirpating that vile race of beings call'd man but I (who you know am clever (VERREE) clever) have thought of an improvement in the sistim suppose we were to Cut of [sic] their *prominent members* and by that means render them Harmless innofencive Little Creatures; We might have such charming *vocal* Music Every house might be Qualified to get up an opera and Piccinis Music would be still more in vogue than it is & we might make such usefull Animals of them in other Respects Consider Well this scheme.

Maria Allen (c. 1750–?), friend and correspondent of Fanny Burney

SWEET REVENGE

"I think there is nothing so pleasant as revenge; I would pursue a man who had injured me to the very brink of life. I know it would be impossible for me ever to forgive him; and I would have him live only that I might have the pleasure of seeing him miserable."

Sarah Fielding (1710–68), English writer, from David Simple

"Aren't men beasts!" cried Lily, banging the imitation-ivory brush in her hand on to the dressing-table. "I'll pay them out some day, see if I don't!"

Ella Hepworth Dixon (1857–1932), English writer, from One Doubtful Hour, and Other Side-Lights on the Feminine Temperament

Don't waste time trying to break a man's heart; be satisfied if you can just manage to chip it in a brand new place.

Helen Rowland (1875–1950), American journalist

I never hated a man enough to give him his diamonds back.

Zsa Zsa Gabor (b. 1919), Hungarian-born American actress

My grandmother was a very tough woman. She buried three husbands. Two of them were just napping.

Rita Rudner (b. 1955), American comedian

"...my husbands have been very unlucky."

Lucrezia Borgia (1480–1519), Italian noblewoman

Sweet Revenge

All over America women are burning dinners.
It's lambchops in Peoria; it's haddock
in Providence; it's steak in Chicago;
tofu delight in Big Sur; red
rice and beans in Dallas.
All over America women are burning
food they're supposed to bring with calico
smile on platters glittering like wax.
Anger sputters in her brainpan, confined
but spewing out missiles of hot fat.
Carbonized despair presses like a clinker
from a barbecue against the back of her eyes.
If she wants to grill anything, it's
her husband spitted over a slow fire.
If she wants to serve him anything
it's a dead rat with a bomb in its belly
ticking like the heart of an insomniac.
Her life is cooked and digested,
nothing but leftovers in
    Tupperware.
Look, she says, once I was
    roast duck
on your platter with parsley
    but now I am Spam.
Burning dinner is not
    incompetence but war.

Marge Piercy (b. 1936), American writer

Francine
immediately began
the business of
not returning
Ralph's call.

Rachel Cusk (b. 1967)
English novelist
from The Temporary

Time wounds all heels

Jane Ace (1905–1974)
American comedian

He cannot even yet think, without a bitter pang, of the woman who had inspired the young man's hysterical tears and sincere, though silly, suicidal impulses. Jim took the pang with him to the Rockies, stinging ... and he has brought it back with him. He packs it into his portmanteau as much as a matter of course as he does his shirts – in fact more so, for he has once inadvertently left his shirts behind, but the pang never.

Rhoda Broughton (1840–1920), English novelist from Alas!

When this judge let a rapist go because the woman had been wearing a miniskirt and so was "asking for it" I thought, ladies, what we all should do is this: next time we see an ugly guy on the street, shoot him. After all, he knew he was ugly when he left the house. He was asking for it.

Ellen Cleghorn, 20th-century American writer and comedian

When your escort passes out in a public place, waste no time worrying over him. Get up and leave quickly; take a taxi and go home. He will find his way home somehow when he comes to or has been thrown out by the management. If you are fond of the young man and don't wish him to get into too much trouble, you might take his money and other valuables before departing, leaving him only taxi fare. If you do this, he won't be able to get into any further mischief when he recovers.

When your companion passes out in a taxi, get out at your own house, give the driver the young man's address, and think no more about him. Of course, if you should be very annoyed, you might tell the driver to take the lad to Yonkers or some obscure spot in Brooklyn.

Alice-Leone Moats (1908–89), American journalist and writer

He still has a lingering sense of discomfort at having availed himself, for his own profit, of her ductility.

Rhoda Broughton (1840–1920) English novelist from Alas!

MANEATERS

SEX

I only like two kinds of men: *domestic* and *imported.*

Mae West (1893–1980), American actress

Man in his lust has regulated long enough this whole question of sexual intercourse. Now let the mother of mankind, whose prerogative it is to set bounds to his indulgence, rouse up and give this whole matter a thorough, fearless examination.

Elizabeth Cady Stanton (1815–1902), American suffragist, abolitionist, historian and writer

Wit in women is apt to have bad consequences; like a sword without a scabbard, it wounds the wearer and provokes assailants. I am sorry to say the generality of women who have excelled in wit have failed in chastity.

Elizabeth Montagu (1720–1800), English essayist and letter writer

In *her* world, men loved women as the fox loves the hare. And women loved men as the tapeworm loves the gut.

Pat Barker (b. 1943), English novelist
from Regeneration

Lady Cathcart, on marrying her fourth husband in 1713, had "If I survive I will have five" engraved upon her wedding ring.

Lady Dorothy Nevill (1826–1913)
English writer and society leader

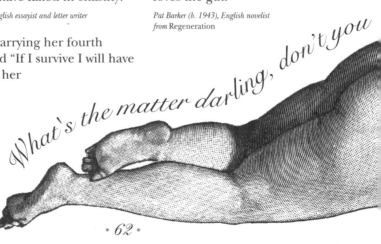

What's the matter darling, don't you

OF THE
JUNGLE

Dolly has a most reprehensible style of dancing... Dolly is the sort of woman, upon whom Mr Algernon Swinburne would write pages of magnificent uncleanness.

Rhoda Broughton (1840–1920), English novelist
from Cometh Up as A Flower

Men aren't attracted to me by my mind. They're attracted by what I don't mind.

Gypsy Rose Lee (1914–70)
American stripper

When women go wrong, men go right after them.

Mae West (1893–1980), American actress

I like to wake up feeling a new man.

Jean Harlow (1911–37)
American actress

recognize me with my clothes on?

Tallulah Bankhead (1902–68), American actress

I feel like a million tonight

Mae West (1893–1980)
American actress

but one at a time

Acknowledgements

extract from *Five Minutes in Heaven* by Lisa Alther reproduced by permission of Dutton Signet, a division of Penguin Books USA Inc. © 1995 by Lisa Alther.

extract from *Kinflicks* by Lisa Alther, published by Alfred A. Knopf, a division of Random House, Inc. © 1975 by Lisa Alther.

extract from *Wilderness Tips* by Margaret Atwood, published by Bloomsbury Publishing. © 1991 by Margaret Atwood.

extract from *The Purveyor of Enchantment* by Marika Cobbold, published by Black Swan, a division of Transworld Publishers Ltd. © 1996 Marika Cobbold.

extracts from *Women Talking Dirty* by Isla Dewar, published by Hodder Headline, reprinted courtesy of Andrew Mann Ltd. and Glenys Bean © 1996 Isla Dewar.

extract from "Seventeen Warnings In Search of a Feminist Poem" from *Becoming Light* by Erica Jong reproduced courtesy of HarperCollins Publishers, Inc. Copyright © 1961, 1962, 1971, 1973, 1975, 1977, 1979, 1981, 1983, 1987, 1991 by Erica Mann Jong.

extract from "Pro-Femina" from *Mermaids in the Basement: Poems for Women* by Carolyn Kizer, published by Copper Canyon Press. © 1991 Carolyn Kizer.

extracts from *No Nice Girl Swears* by Alice-Leone Moats, published by Cassell and Company in 1933. Reprinted by permission of McIntosh & Otis, Inc.

"For Willyce" from *Movement in Black Ithaca* by Pat Parker, reprinted with permission from Firebrand Books, Ithaca. © 1978 Pat Parker.

"Why Dorothy Wordsworth is Not as Famous as Her Brother", by Lynn Peters, first published in *Cosmopolitan,* reproduced courtesy of the author. © 1991 Lynn Peters.

"What's that smell in the kitchen?" by Marge Piercy reproduced courtesy of A M Heath & Co. © 1980, 1982, 1983 and 1995 by Marge Piercy and Middlemarsh, Inc.

extract from *The Visitation* by Sue Reidy published by Black Swan, a division of Transword Publishers Ltd. © 1996 Sue Reidy.

"A Song of White Hair" by Chuo Wên-chũn from *The Orchid Boat, Women Poets of China,* edited by Kenneth Rexroth and Ling Chung. © 1972 by Kenneth Rexroth and Ling Chung. Reprinted by permission of the Continuum Publishing Company.

Every effort has been made to locate copyright-holders. In the event that we have unwillingly or inadvertently omitted the proper notification, the editor would be grateful to hear from the copyright-holder and undertakes to amend any subsequent edition of this title accordingly.